RIVERS AND STREAMS

JENNY VAUGHAN

HODDER
Wayland

an imprint of Hodder Children's Books

GEOGRAPHY STARTS HERE!

Rivers and Streams

OTHER TITLES IN THE SERIES
**Maps and Symbols · Hills and Mountains
Weather Around You · Where People Live
Your Environment**

**Produced for Wayland Publishers Limited by
Lionheart Books
10, Chelmsford Square
London NW10 3AR
England**

Designer: Ben White

Editor: Lionel Bender

Picture Research: Madeleine Samuel

Electronic make-up: Mike Pilley, Radius

Illustrated by Rudi Visi and Peter Bull

**First published in Great Britain in 1997
by Wayland (Publishers) Ltd**

**Reprinted in 2001 by Hodder Wayland,
an imprint of Hodder Children's Books**

British Library Cataloguing in Publication Data
Vaughan, Jenny,

Rivers and streams. – (Geography starts here!)

1. Rivers– Juvenile literature

I. Title II. Bender, Lionel

551.4'83

ISBN 0 7502 3407 5
Printed and bound by L.E.G.O. S.p.A., Vicenza, Italy

Picture Acknowledgements
Pages 1: Wayland Publishers Limited. 5, 7: GeoScience Features.
8-9: Zefa- Stockmarket. 9: Lionheart Books. 10: James Davis Travel
Photography. 11: Lionheart Books. 13: Kalt/Zefa. 14: Zefa/Ikholm.
15: James Davis Travel Photography. 16: Lionheart Books.
17: Wayland Publishers Limited. 18: Zefa/Damm. 19, 20, 24, 27, 31:
Wayland Publishers Limited. 21: Zefa. 22: Zefa/Ung. Werbestudio.
25: Zefa. 26-27: Zefa/Aiken. 28: David Simson/DAS Photos.
29: Zefa/Stockmarket. Cover: Zefa.

The photo on the previous page shows traditional sailboats on the River Nile in Egypt.

CONTENTS

RAIN AND RIVERS

Rivers begin as rain falling on high ground or water from melting snow. The water flows downhill as little streams. These meet and join together to form a broad river, flowing towards the sea.

The journey of a river from its source (where it starts) to the sea can be thousands of kilometres long. The place where it flows into the sea is called its mouth.

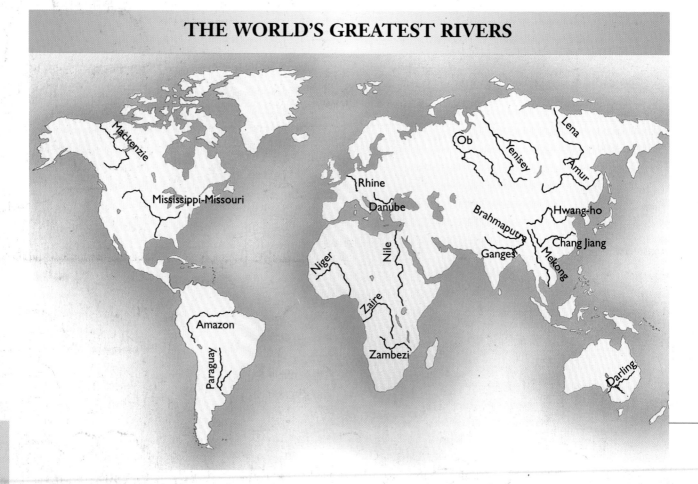

THE WORLD'S GREATEST RIVERS

The start of the Rhône River in Switzerland. Streams flow from the end of the melting Rhône Glacier.

THE PARTS OF A RIVER

Stream water flows from melting snow in mountains in Norway.

Some rivers start where rain water that has collected under the ground bubbles to the surface. This is called a spring. Others start from mountain bogs. These soak up rain water, which then seeps out as a stream.

Rivers also start from masses of ice called glaciers. These form on high, cold mountain slopes. At the bottom end of a glacier the ice melts and water gushes away as a stream, or little river.

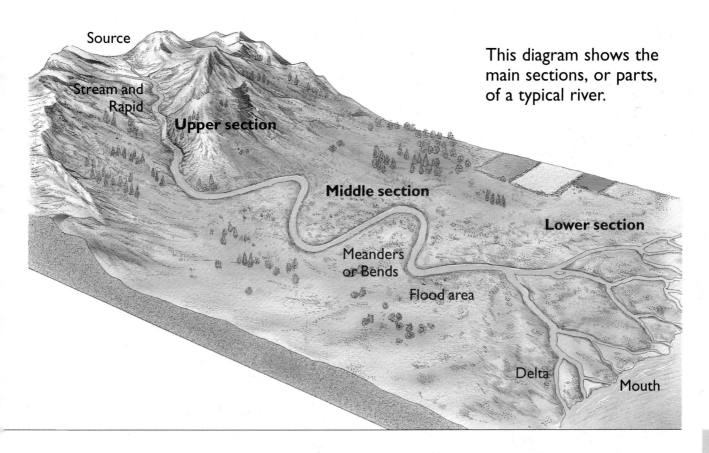

Source

Stream and Rapid

Upper section

Middle section

Meanders or Bends

Flood area

Lower section

Delta

Mouth

This diagram shows the main sections, or parts, of a typical river.

Streams and Rapids

As a stream tumbles downhill, the rushing water carries along rocks and stones. These crash together and break up into gravel, sand and mud. As more streams join together, a river forms.

A river may flow underground, carving out caves in the rock. Or it may flow over lumps of rock that are in its way. This creates a shallow, fast-flowing part of the river called a rapid.

SPEED OF FLOW

Drop two small sticks into a river in different places – one in the middle of the river, the other close to the bank.

Do they both travel at the same speed?

Warning

NEVER play near water unless there is an adult to look after you.

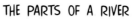

Children play with sticks in the water of a fast-flowing stream. A flow of water is known as a current.

▼A stream flows through a narrow channel in rocks. The sides of the channel have been worn away by river water.

The Middle of a River

Sometimes, a river drops straight down a steep slope. This creates a waterfall. The water crashes into a deep pool at the bottom of the slope, where it swirls about in dangerous currents.

As a river reaches flatter ground, it flows more slowly. Loose gravel and sand carried along by water currents falls to the bed, or bottom, of the river.

The middle of the Amazon River in South America. This river flows through the largest rain forest in the world.

River

Fall

Hard rock

Deep pool

Soft rock, easily worn away by river

This diagram shows a cut-away section of a typical waterfall.

The Niagara Falls between Canada and the USA. The falling water makes a thick cloud of spray.

Flood Areas

On very flat land, a river flows extremely slowly and winds from side to side like a snake moving over the ground.

Heavy rain or a sudden thaw of snow can cause a slow-flowing river to fill with too much water. Then, water spills out of the river on to the land, causing a flood.

People living in flood areas sometimes build high banks called levees along a river's edge to try to stop water spilling over.

Here you can see how a river bend is left behind as a river changes course. The bend becomes an ox-bow lake.

Currents wear away one bank of a river (blue arrow) and drop loose sand and gravel on the opposite bank (red arrow).

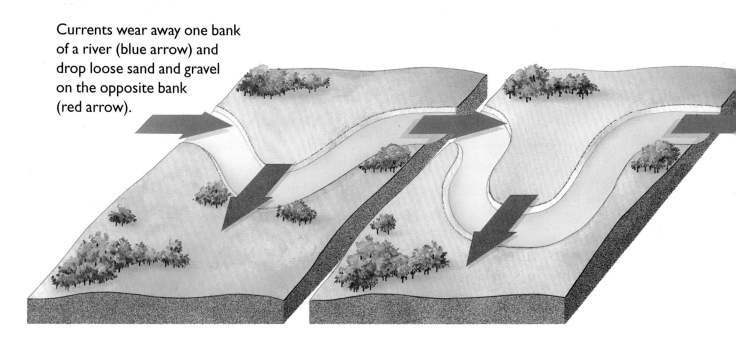

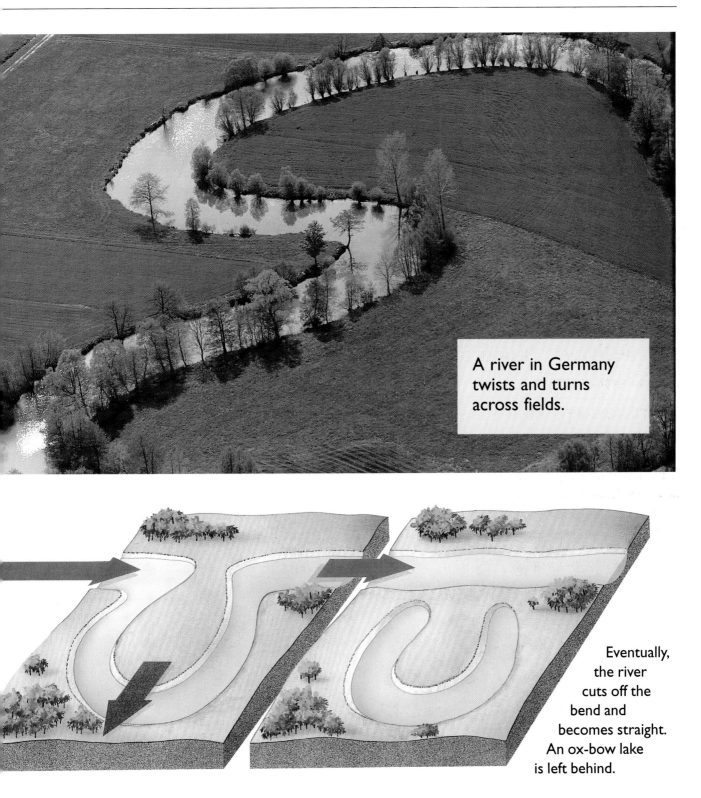

A river in Germany twists and turns across fields.

Eventually, the river cuts off the bend and becomes straight. An ox-bow lake is left behind.

The delta of the Okavango River, in Botswana.

Deltas and Estuaries

A river flows into the sea in one of two ways. The first is as an estuary. Here, the mouth of the river gradually gets wider and more open.

The second way is as a delta. Mud and sand carried along by the river form islands near the sea. The river water flows round the islands to form a pattern like the branches of a tree.

A man paddles his small boat across the huge Amazon River in Brazil.

PEOPLE AND RIVERS

Rivers can be used to carry goods and people from place to place. Before there were roads and railways, rivers were the main routes of travel. This is why many towns are near rivers.

In many countries, people use the same river water for washing, drinking and getting rid of human waste. This spreads the germs that cause diseases such as cholera and typhoid. It is important to keep river water clean.

Manhattan Island, New York, is between the mouths of two rivers – the Hudson River and the East River.

People bathe in the Ganges River in India as part of their Hindu religious customs.

Farmers in Egypt use a pump to raise water from a canal that brings water from the Nile River.

Water for Farms

Farmers use rivers to water their crops.
They dig channels and use machines to get
the water from rivers and on to the land.
This is known as irrigation.

Most farmers use fertilizers, or chemicals,
to help grow their crops. But the chemicals
wash into rivers where they may kill animals.

A farmer in China digs a
canal in order to irrigate,
or bring water to his land,
from a nearby river.

Shipping Routes

Some rivers are wide and deep enough for large ships to sail on them. The ships carry goods to and from factories along the river.

Boats and ferries carry people and cars along rivers. Bridges built across rivers must be tall enough to let ships and boats pass under them.

These people are leaving a ferryboat station. Ferries sail along the Volga River in Russia every day.

Pleasure boats carry sightseers on the Seine River in Paris, France.

Looking down on a
river from the top of
a dam in India.

Power from Rivers

Rivers can power machines. Flowing water can turn waterwheels. The wheels turn large, flat stones to grind corn.

Rivers can also be used to make electricity. Water is made to run through huge waterwheels called turbines. As these turn, they produce electricity for use in homes, offices and factories.

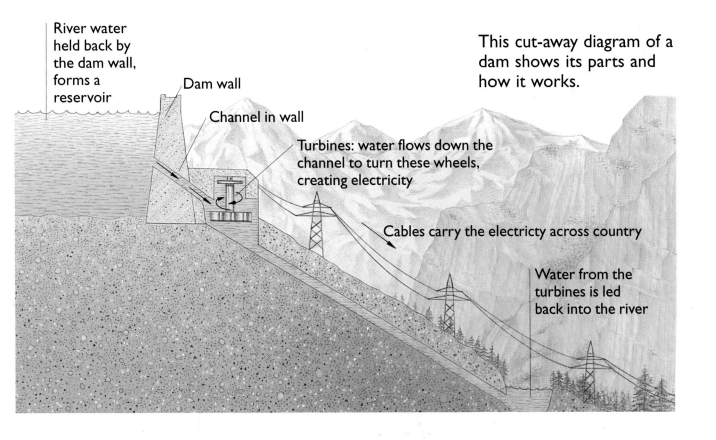

River water held back by the dam wall, forms a reservoir

Dam wall

Channel in wall

This cut-away diagram of a dam shows its parts and how it works.

Turbines: water flows down the channel to turn these wheels, creating electricity

Cables carry the electricty across country

Water from the turbines is led back into the river

RIVERS AND NATURE

All plants need water, but some only grow well in or near rivers. Riverside plants include irises, reeds and rushes, and some kinds of trees.

Plants that grow in fast-flowing water have strong roots to cling to the river bed. Where water is slow-moving, plants such as water lilies grow, with leaves that float on the surface. Some weeds grow completely underwater.

A fisherman in a boat among reeds in the Danube River, in Europe.

Weeds and algae can choke slow-flowing rivers so that the fish in them cannot breathe and die.

River Animals

Rivers are home to all kinds of animals. Trout and salmon live in fast-flowing streams. Other fish, such as perch, prefer slow-moving water. So do frogs and toads.

Many fish are eaten by river birds, such as kingfishers and herons, or by alligators.

Dragonflies, gnats and other insects spend the first part of their lives in slow-moving water. They leave it when they are adults.

A female hippopotamus and her baby stand on a riverbank in Zambia.

LIFE IN A STREAM

You can see some of the small animals that live in rivers by collecting a sample of water from a slow-flowing stream.

Use a glass or plastic jar to scoop up some water from the shallows near the stream bank. You may see snails, insects, water spiders and small fish.

When you have finished, gently pour the water back into the stream.

An alligator rests on a bank of the Amazon River.

DISASTERS!

Many of the world's rivers are in danger. Chemicals from farms and factories are washed into them, making the water poisonous. People are trying to clean rivers so that plants and animals return to them.

Rivers can also cause dangers. Floods can wash away homes, farms, roads, railways and bridges. People and animals can also be killed in serious floods.

Roads, fields and a small island lie under water after the flood of a river in northern France.

Trees and mud baked dry by sunshine in a dried-up river bed in Sardinia.

RIVER FACTS AND FIGURES

The world's longest rivers
Nile 6,695 kilometres.
Amazon 6,516 kilometres.
Yangtze 6,380 kilometres.
Mississippi 6,019 kilometres.
Ob 5,570 kilometres.

It is not always possible to say exactly where a river begins. Some books will give different figures for the lengths of the world's rivers.

The world's biggest river
The Amazon contains one-fifth of all the river water in the world.

The highest waterfall
The Salto Angel (Angel Falls) in Venezuela, South America, is the highest waterfall in the world, at 979 metres.

Other amazing waterfalls
The Boyama Falls in Zaire carry 17,000 cubic metres of water a second – more than any other waterfall.

Victoria Falls, on the Zambezi River in southern Africa, sends up so much spray that some days the falls can be seen from a distance of 40 kilometres away.

The world's largest delta
This is where the Ganges and the Brahmaputra rivers meet and flow into the sea along the coast of India and Bangladesh. The delta covers an area of 109,000 square kilometres – bigger than many countries in the world.

An unusual delta
The Okavango River, in southern Africa, ends in a delta where the water sinks into the sands of the Kalahari Desert. The river never reaches the sea.

The biggest dam
The Grand Coulee Dam in Washington State in the USA is 167 metres high and 1,272 metres long.

The worst flood ever
This happened in China in 1877. The Hwang-ho River flooded and killed nearly a million people.

Further Reading

Exploring Water Habitats CD-Rom (Wayland, 1997)

Flood, The Violent Earth series, by Julia Waterlow (Wayland, 1992)

Junior Education Volume 17, issue no. 5 (May 1993) includes a Focus Pack on Rivers, by Bill Chambers and Jane De'ath.

The Mississippi, The World's Rivers series, by Nina Morgan, (Wayland, 1992)

River, Land Shapes series, by Brian Knapp (Atlantic Europe Children's Books, 1992)

Rivers, Ponds and Lakes, Ecology Watch series, by Anita Ganeri (Cloverleaf, 1991)

The Thames, The Amazon, River Journeys series, by David Cumming (Wayland, 1994, 1995)

GLOSSARY

Algae Tiny green plants. Most of them live in water.

Bogs Wet, spongy ground.

Cholera A dangerous disease caused by germs that spread through water.

Currents Movements of water.

Fertilizers Chemicals that are added to soil to help plants grow.

Flood When there is so much water in a river that it flows over the banks and covers the surrounding land.

Glacier A river of ice that forms from snow in hollows on mountains.

Irrigation Supplying water to farm land, often by building canals and ditches.

Levees Banks, or walls of earth, built by people to keep a river from flooding over the surrounding land.

Mouth The place where a river flows into the sea – or, sometimes, into a lake.

Rapids Fast-flowing, shallow parts of a river.

Spring A small stream which springs up out of the ground.

Turbines Machines that are turned by flowing water, steam or gas.

Typhoid A dangerous disease spread by dirty water.

Waterfall A place where a stream or river falls over a cliff.

A river bend in France.

INDEX